App and Datacenter Modernization – The Evolutionary Step in I.T. Optimization
Mini-Book Strategy Series – Book 4

Authors: Rand Morimoto, Ph.D., MCSE
&
Chris Amaris, MCITP, CISSP

DEDICATION

I dedicate this book to my kids Noble, Kelly, Chip,
and Eduardo - Rand Morimoto

I dedicate this book Sophia and our 5 children, Michelle, Megan, Zoe,
Zachary, and Ian. - Chris Amaris

ACKNOWLEDGMENTS

Thank you to all of our clients whom we've worked with over the past 4-years modernizing their applications and laying the foundation of the best practices that we share with others today. What works best always starts with early adopters and strategic implementers, and we've been fortunate to have many organizations that have leveraged the latest technologies to formulate a definitive process of what works and what doesn't. The results of these efforts is what has been provided in the pages of this book.

TABLE OF CONTENTS

INTRODUCTION

It has become clear that Cloud Technologies are not a short term fad nor technological solution relegated to a small subset of business solutions. Rather, cloud applications like email in the cloud leveraging Microsoft's Office 365 or Google for Business, or client relationship management in the cloud with Salesforce.com, and even datacenter solutions utilizing Amazon AWS and Microsoft Azure have become mainstream core business solutions.

As organizations plan out their 12, 18, and 24 month I.T. plans, technology architects have to consider cloud solutions as a probable fit for their business needs. However, the focus of this book is not on "migrating to the cloud," but rather "modernizing Applications and the Datacenter." The difference is focusing on updating internal I.T. technologies that leverage the best near term and long term solutions available, than simply believing that everything needs to go to the cloud.

What we've found over the years is that the Cloud does provide some very good solutions and benefits for organizations. Microsoft's Office 365 email and Salesforce.com are good examples of solutions that work better as hosted shared services than what a typical organization can afford to implement, manage, and support on their own.

There are many solutions that organizations have moved to the cloud however that all they've done is bundle up a relatively ineffective solution on-premise, and moved that inefficient application to run in the cloud as a hosted virtual machine. Same application, same problems and inefficiencies, but just running in a different datacenter environment.

The focus of this book is to provide best practices and lessons learned in building the strategy to modernize organization's applications and datacenter operations to take advantage of the most appropriate solution available. The solution may be a cloud-based application, or the solution may be an on-premise solution. This book will provide guidance on the decision points and best practices in developing the modernization strategy.

1 IDENTIFYING THE NEED FOR CHANGE

The technology industry tends to introduce a major new model of computing every 5-7 years, and goes through significant changes every 12-15 years. The recent 5-7 year changes have included the introduction of the smart phone and tablet to the compute environment, along with mobile and web applications. The major changes over the decades have been the evolution of centralized mainframe computing to desktop local area network attached computing to mobile and cloud-based computing.

This latest evolutionary change of cloud-based and mobile-device based computing has now taken hold, and enterprises are now looking to fully develop their strategy to integrate core cloud and mobile technologies in their workforce environment.

Legacy Targeting of Buying, Building, and Running Systems

For many, the idea of changing a well-developed and proven I.T. strategy to something new or different is challenging. We have spent years developing a process that now works extremely well. We buy, build, and run systems that has reliably kept the I.T. services in our organizations running for years.

This new model of cloud services removes the buy, build, and run process from our internal I.T. personnel, and requires us to rely on someone else to maintain the critical I.T. services for our organizations. Mobile computing extends the security of our organizations beyond the desktops and laptop systems that we've gotten good at locking down and managing.

However, cloud and mobile computing has proven why this buy, build, and run model is no longer the most efficient or effective business model for organizations today and into the future.

I.T. Like the Package Delivery Industry

A common analogy used to describe the dramatic changes being undertaken in the changes in the technology industry is a comparison with the product and package delivery industry. Years ago, if you manufactured a product in a small town, you would package the product up, put it on one of your trucks, and deliver it to the marketplace or to your customers directly. As the organization grew, the business would buy a bigger truck or more trucks to move their goods around.

This do-it-yourself shipping model worked great when the organization was able to string together marketplaces and routes that made the delivery of their goods efficient. However, as the organization expanded to new markets, with ups and downs in deliveries to small marketplaces or individuals across the country or around the globe, the do-it-yourself shipping model was no longer effective.

However, in the past 3 decades, package shipping organizations like UPS and FedEx came about that allowed an organization to ship 1 item, 5 items, 500 items to virtually any marketplace. Organizations were able to effectively shift the reliance of one of the most critical aspects of their business (the delivery of their products) to another organization who was better setup and more efficiently delivered their products.

These package delivery companies allowed organizations to get out of the shipping and transportation logistics business, and refocus on their core product and services. The package delivery companies were better focused at optimizing transportation costs, served great marketplaces, and more efficiently fulfilled on a key components of organizations in the final delivery of their products.

Cloud computing has also transformed the delivery of application functionality to be an optimized service model than a do-it-yourself model. While early providers of cloud services did not have the discipline or rigor for reliability and security, nor the scale to optimize the cost of the service, we're now at a point where core cloud providers are integral in providing key business services just like UPS and FedEx are depended on for providing key product delivery services.

Optimized for Self-Sufficiency

Just as the analogy describes a clear example of an optimized operational model for shared services, it becomes more and more clear how I.T. organizations have built out a business model of extreme self-sufficiency that is the clear driving force of why change is needed in the industry.

I.T. best practices over the past decade have developed a model where each and every I.T. organization created their own datacenters built on internal systems that had layers of security and redundancy. When the public power grid wasn't sufficient enough in terms of power reliability, battery backup systems were put in place to maintain system operations. When battery backup systems weren't sufficient enough to maintain the operations of the I.T. systems during an extended outage, diesel generators were added to the operational datacenters. And when a single site wasn't sufficient enough in the event of a site failure, all of the business systems were replicated in a redundant datacenter with self-sufficiency built into that redundant center to maintain operations.

I.T. best practices over the past several years has meant every organization's I.T. department had to be independently ready to withstand the 30-year flood, the once in a lifetime earthquake, and the traumatic shutdown of the power grid.

Internalizing the Cost of High Availability and Disaster Recovery

As touched on in the last section, every single organization has been building their I.T. operations with self-sufficiency, including high availability and disaster recovery built in to their operations. When one is good, two is better, and three is even better than that. It's not necessarily "I.T.'s fault" for this level of redundancy as every I.T. organization has experience being "yelled at" when a system is down and the organization is losing "millions of dollars a day" because of the failure. It has been I.T. managements responsibility to "do whatever is necessary" to ensure the core business systems are operational 24 x 7 x 365.

However, it is this internalization of cost of this high availability and disaster recovery that has made basic I.T. services so expensive for each organization to fulfill on their own. We've finally crossed that barrier where the value provided by I.T. doesn't completely match the extreme cost it takes to provide the services when other alternatives, like cloud services, have become available that provide organizations an alternative to their internal services.

Back to the analogy of the business person shipping and delivering his own goods, while he was making a certain type of widget to sell to customers, a major portion of the business investment went into the delivery trucks to deliver the goods, and the spare trucks and spare truck drivers standing by just in case the primary trucks and drivers were unable to fulfill on deliveries, and a third spare of trucks and drivers in case a localized event prevented the primary and secondary trucks and drivers from fulfilling on their responsibilities. All of this investment placed in the delivery of basic services that have nothing to do with the core line of business for the organization.

When Overhead Exceeds the Facility for Utility

And the last piece on this commentary on why a change in I.T. is needed is around the general overhead that it takes to run application services for an organization. This has become very evident in organizations that have moved most or all of their applications to a cloud-based model. What is left in these organizations are dozens of servers and systems of "management systems". Things like domain controllers, DNS name servers, DHCP servers, patching servers, software deployment servers, backup servers, monitoring servers, intrusion detection servers, management console servers for each application, management console servers for the management system, etc, etc, etc.

As organizations have optimized their applications and datacenter operations, the number of servers and systems leftover to simply run and manage the management systems showed how much overhead exists in datacenters today to simply provide basic application services.

We'll get into more specifics in subsequent chapters, and how to best optimize I.T. operations today and in the near future to truly improve and modernize application and datacenter operations.

2 CLOUD BROUGHT ABOUT BETTER WAYS OF DOING I.T.

Cloud provided services are no different than any other specialized operational service. The more you do of it, the better you get at it. And if it is your line of business that your organization will make or break based on its success, then the efficiencies and effectiveness of the service will be optimized over time. Just as each enterprise has individually developed and optimized its I.T. operations multiplied by the hundreds and thousands of organizations doing the same thing worldwide, cloud providers simply extend the volume, capacity, scale, and efficiencies to extend their services to support hundreds of thousands and millions of users.

Paying for Services You Use

Cloud services have been about paying for services you use, just like the package shipping industry that allows you to pay for 1-day, 2-day, 3-day shipping times, add in insurance options, and add-in specialty services like morning delivery, Saturday delivery, proof of delivery, and the like. The whole concept is that you pick and choose what you want to buy, pay for those services, and choose to have some services one way, and other services another.

The application cloud service industry will still see a shake-up in this type of services arrangement, just as every other service industry ultimately optimizes to an a la carte in addition to their bundled offerings. Today, the nature of most cloud service providers is to bundle together more and more services, thus raising the "value" and the cost of their bundled services for things you may or may not want. Pricing models have remained the same over the past 3-4 years more than have dropped through what would be expected over time, however as other providers enter the market and provide more a la carte services, we'll eventually see more competitive individualized pricing.

This is similar to the mobile phone service industry where mobile phone prices have gone up over time as providers bundle in more data services, unlimited nationwide calling, "friends and family" plans, and the like. However, with pressure from Internet-based telephony providers (like Google Hangouts, Office 365 Cloud PBX, Skype, Viber, WhatsApp, etc) and metropolitan area WiFi service providers, the traditional mobile phone carriers are unbundling services and working to compete for business again.

Bottomline, cloud services open the way for individuals and organizations to pay for services and eventually only the services they use and need.

Economies of Scale

Ultimately, the business model for cloud is an Economics 101 "economies of scale" model. A consolidated organization doing the same thing for a thousand companies should be able to do it more efficiently and effectively than a thousand companies each doing the same thing on their own. Because an organization whose sole business is to provide reliable, secure, and effective services is dependent on that quality of service, they will be driven to invest at levels to ensure they will retain the trust of their customers and ultimately maintain their customer base, if not expand their customer base from their quality and reputation. Just as internal I.T. organizations have invested in server redundancy, storage redundancy, and site redundancy, so will the cloud hosted providers.

However, unlike a thousand organizations each building out this redundancy and reliability for just their organization, the cloud provider will spread this redundancy, security, and operational cost across hundreds or thousands of companies, thus ultimately driving costs down, while driving reliability and security up.

OpEx vs CapEx

The cloud services model changes the cost model for organizations from one of major expenditures that are Capital Expenses (CapEx) of hardware, software, and datacenter infrastructure costs, to that of a monthly Operational Expense (OpEx) model. As much as I.T. budgets have been typically consistent with a base cost plus typically an annual cost increase each year, inside each I.T. budget are large swings in major upgrade expenses that have been staggered over 2-3 years. Organizations have picked a handful of their applications to upgrade every year, rotating out the upgrades in these 2-3 year cycles, whether it's a major email system upgrade every 3-5 years, or the purchase of a new Enterprise Resource Planning (ERP) system or Accounting software system every 5-7 years, or a major upgrade of a database system every 2-3 years. Organizations have had major outlays in capital purchases to maintain the operations of their reliable and secure I.T. environments.

The shift from hardware and software purchases to a subscription model common of cloud services shifts the budgeting from staggered major expenditures to a regular monthly cost. Organizations can now calculate a monthly cost of application services on a per employee basis. Financially, this subscription model shifts organizations into an operational expense model instead of a capital expense model, and provides organization the ability to more easily budget for I.T. expenses based on these monthly subscription fees.

Bypassing Cloud Wannabe's

In the early days of cloud and application services, it was difficult for I.T. executives and personnel to truly depend on the reliability, security, integrity, and dependability of the cloud providers. There was a period where anyone and everyone in the I.T. industry overnight became a "cloud provider". While their product hadn't changed, all of a sudden their applications were marketed as "ready for the cloud." The reality is the same application built for a 1000-person company was now being touted as an application that could scale and support 100,000 or a million users. These "wannabe cloud providers" gave the entire sector a bad reputation when the early clouds failed for hours or days, had security breaches, or didn't provide the level of price/value that was touted by the provider.

While not to say that all of these wannabe cloud providers are gone, enough major cloud providers have matured and are now on their second, third, or fourth generation of software, built specific for cloud scale, cloud security, and cloud reliability. These mature cloud providers have improved if not perfected their models for rolling upgrades and updates, defense in depth security, and operational efficiencies.

As the competitive nature of the market economy eliminates inefficient and ineffective service providers, greater confidence can be placed in the surviving organizations servicing the marketplace.

Consolidated Investments and Expertise

Over the past few years as cloud providers have evolved their product and service offerings, a clear consolidation of investments and expertise into a defined set of providers has taken place. Instead of email system experts in every single company in the world managing their own messaging system, the top email experts have consolidated into working at or working with the major cloud-messaging and communication platform hosted providers.

Instead of every organization having their own internal security experts that span 20-30 core business applications, each organization now has their security experts focused on 5-10 core internal business applications, with oversight of the security of their hosted cloud applications. A greater number of security experts now work within the hosted cloud provider organizations doing internal security for the major cloud providers, as well as third party security experts performing external audits, reviews, assessments, and support of the major cloud providers.

The industry still needs experts and top run operations, however the experts are consolidated into fewer individual organizations, with a similar consolidation of investments in these I.T. operations serving millions and tens of millions of users, not simply hundreds and thousands of users.

When Cloud Scale Equates to Cloud Reliability

And lastly, cloud scale means that hosted cloud providers have a true investment in their operational success that is dependent the reliability of services to their customers. Just like if a package delivery company lost packages or was not dependable in delivering packages on time as expected, the organization wouldn't stay in business very long.

Cloud scale with the consolidation of investments and expertise has taken operational reliability to a higher level. I.T. organizations for years have touted their uptime as 99.99% or 99.999%, but effectively cheated in their calculations. For example, most organizations have not counted "planned downtime" in their uptime numbers. If they do system maintenance every 2 weeks, and everyone in the organization knows that the maintenance will be happening, that would not count against the organizations uptime statistics. For internal organizations, they would be able to pick a time that is convenient for the organization where this planned downtime could take place (weekend, evening, middle of a quarter, etc).

Other organizations have completely cheated the statistics by deferring all maintenance, upgrades, or even server reboots to report they have had NO downtime. We've seen some organizations run 2-3 years without doing any system maintenance, which sounds great when they can tout 99.999% uptime, but eventually the systems do fail, and in many cases the servers don't even come back online and the organization suffers several days of unplanned outage time.

However, in the cloud environment, an evening or weekend for a traditional business may be a perfect time for planned downtime, however for an organization servicing the public during weekends or evenings, or emergency services organizations servicing the public 24 hours a day, 7-days a week would find that evening and weekend cloud disruption to be significant. As such, true cloud providers have no "good time for planned downtime," and cloud providers typically calculate a true uptime metric that includes planned and unplanned outages.

Thus, the key hosted cloud providers have developed processes that allow them to "roll out" upgrades and updates across all users and organizations without bringing the service to a halt. Cloud scale has truly produced cloud reliability as a key tenet in defining a long term successful hosted cloud provider.

CLOUD BROUGHT ABOUT BETTER WAYS OF DOING I.T.

3 THE HYBRID STRATEGY – NOT JUST MIGRATING TO THE CLOUD

As much as the first couple chapters of this book have focused on talking about hosted cloud applications, or cloud computing, in reality, the cloud is just ONE option for the target destination of application modernization. Just as the title of this book denotes, the goal is application and datacenter modernization, not cloud migration. A hybrid strategy that includes some applications that remain on-premise, and some applications that are migrated to the cloud have been found to be the norm for organizations modernization their I.T. operations.

Cloud as an Option, Not the Total End Goal

The end goal for any I.T. organization is to truly optimize their I.T. operations. In basic economic terms, I.T. should leverage the most efficient and effective services that fulfill on the business requirements of the organization at an optimized cost. Early cloud solutions did not meet the security or reliability requirements of many organizations, and thus 2 or 3 years ago, the cloud wasn't the best solution for many of these organizations. However, over time, the cloud providers have improved and optimized their services, and are now providing mature, highly secure, and reliable services that organizations have to seriously consider as part of their application modernization initiatives.

Many organizations have tried to bundle up their existing highly customized applications, forklift them into the cloud, and then run them in a cloud hosted environment only to find that the cost of running the application isn't cheaper and in many cases significantly more expensive to run a specific application outside of the internal datacenter. In those cases, cloud was not the best choice for a cost or performance perspective. There are several factors in assessing the true efficiencies of the application and datacenter modernization plan that are highlighted throughout the text of this book.

Focusing on App and Datacenter Modernization

When the title of this book "Application and Datacenter Modernization" is clearly defined, it's not about taking 100% of everything being run on-premise today and moving of it to the cloud. The focus on modernization is to clearly assess the use of the application, preferably working from the perspective of the users themselves to determine WHAT the users can most effectively use in their day to day responsibilities.

In early engagements in Application and Datacenter Modernization efforts, in some cases it was found that many employees don't find the applications they are using particularly helpful in completing the tasks of their jobs. Whether that application is on-premise or in the cloud, an ineffective application is an ineffective application for these users. When the day to day tasks of a user is assessed and analyzed, a completely different application is found to be more applicable for those users.

In some cases, the idea of "modernization" has been to completely replace an existing on-premise application with a completely new and different application. In other cases, a Software as a Service (SaaS) application exists that the users are able to take advantage of that is immediately available and provides significant value to the users. Key SaaS examples include accounting applications, client relationship management applications, and human resource management applications.

Many organizations have been using the same accounting software for years, repeatedly upgrading the software every 5-10 years, but finding the function of the general ledger, accounts payable application, and accounts receivable application being sufficient for the organization. However key integration components like time and billing systems, expense report systems, client management systems, project costing, and cost accounting systems integrated into the application are frequently found to be grossly inadequate. The modern SaaS applications have evolved to provide extensive features and functions that enable employees using tablets or mobile phones to quickly enter their timesheets or file expense reports without having to sit in front of a "computer" and a legacy "web browser", instead getting key components of their work done from a readily available mobile app.

It's this type of thinking, assessment, analysis, and business optimization that truly modernizes how organizations improve their business bottom-line. It's that shift from a legacy on-premise application to do the same thing in the cloud that might be more up to date, more functional, and easier to support that is advancing the organization into a modern application environment.

The On-Premise Model for Legacy Applications

One key example of applications remaining on-premise rather than being simply migrated to the cloud are very old customized legacy applications. Some organizations have spent months updating the code or rewriting their legacy applications to support a cloud-model without a lot of thought into understanding how the application is used, and whether the application in its legacy form (now migrated to the cloud) actually serves the organization.

Instead, the application should be assessed, users of the application interviewed to determine "who" uses the application, "what" they use the application for, and "whether" the application actually serves a valuable function to the organization. Or could the same function and utility be achieved with a different application altogether?

With all the applications a typical organization has, it is these old legacy applications that are frequently best off being assessed and dealt with last. The organization can gain more traction and better time utilization by focusing on other applications that may be more effectively migrated to the cloud or modernized, and circle back to these legacy applications later.

These legacy applications may be good candidates to just continue to have them run on-premise, and thus a clear justification of a hybrid model where applications are migrated to the cloud, modernized to a new model, or just left on-premise as the near term strategy of the organization.

Potentially Migrating Core Secure Apps Last

Another key set of applications that are best to leave on-premise are applications that have extremely high security or regulatory compliance requirements wrapped around the application. Rather than spending months trying to create the ultimate secure cloud environment, an organization can better allocate their time and efforts identifying and migrating "all the other applications" in the enterprise that are easier or cleaner to modernize and migrate, and leave the more complex or compliance-restricted applications on-premise to be the last to deal with in modernizing and migrating.

This strategy has proven successful for enterprises as they move email, file collaboration, backup systems, intranet content, accounting software, and the like to cloud-based systems, gain experience with the cloud providers for their reliability and security features, and then make more informed and easier decisions down the line on core specialized applications.

The Larger the Enterprise, the More Likely the Hybrid Model for I.T.

Small organizations with fewer than 300 employees have been successful in modernizing almost "all" of their application and datacenter services into the cloud within a few months with the initial migration of core business productivity applications to Office 365. Subsequent migrations have included initiatives to move the accounting and line of business applications to a SaaS or IaaS VM-based cloud model, and finally leveraging hosted endpoint and server management tools thereafter. But the larger the enterprise, the longer it will take to modernize and optimize applications and the datacenter. It's clear that the modernization process could take months or even years to complete and, as such, a hybrid model is the norm for these larger enterprises.

A huge challenge for large enterprises is simply getting around to all of the application owners across hundreds of applications to do the business analysis assessment of who uses the application, what the application is used for, and whether there is a better way of handling the application with an off the shelf SaaS application, a refactor to a PaaS application, the simple migration of the application to an IaaS virtual machine in the cloud, or whether the application should just remain on-premise.

However, despite the fact that larger enterprises are more complicated and will take longer to modernize their applications and datacenters, this doesn't mean that the large enterprises cannot benefit from the cloud economies of scale. Quite the contrary, the larger the enterprise, the more inefficiencies exist in terms of duplication of similar application function and services, or simply just the operations, support, and management of "systems" that are either under-utilized or even not used at all. In one environment assessment, it was found that of the 480 applications identified by the organization, 120 of the applications were running on servers, backed up daily, and configured for replication and high availability, yet NO users actually used the applications any longer.

So an analysis and assessment for organizations of all sizes nets out a significant benefit simply by optimizing I.T. operations and business services to meet the current needs of the organization.

Planned and Coordinated Transitions to Modernization

We've likened Application and Datacenter Modernization efforts to the work done almost a couple decades ago in Y2K assessments, where every application in the organization is identified, key application owners are identified, and the purpose and use of the application identified. In a very methodical process, an organization can quickly identify how application and datacenter modernization can be conducted in the organization, with categorization of applications that will be the easiest to modernize, versus applications that fit in the category of not appropriate to modernize (or be prioritized last), and everything in-between.

This planned and coordinated transition process can take an organization months or even years to complete, with some logical milestones that include modernizing an application during a typical migration or upgrade cycle. So if an application is upgraded every 4-years and the 4th year comes along, rather than just upgrading the application to the next on-premise version, instead take that opportunity to assess and modernize the application.

Without additional cost, effort, or commitment to time historically allocated for application upgrades and updates, the organization can more rapidly transition to newer, more appropriate and effective applications. The next chapter gets into more specific details on how the assessment is done, and how the transition process is typically completed.

4 FOCUSING ON THE APPLICATION, NOT THE SERVER

So far we've identified the impetus to modernize applications and the datacenter, and when modernization might not be applicable or better deferred. Now we'll get deeper in the assessment and costing process that will help prioritize and justify the strategy and execution of the modernization process.

Over Emphasis on I.T. Infrastructure

One of the first steps in developing a strong strategy to modernize applications and the datacenter model is to separate oneself from the entrenched personal investment in the current I.T. model and methods of service delivery. By starting with a completely new slate in planning the future I.T. model, the architecture can be based on what is best for the organization, and not try to work backwards into making the future I.T. model fit into the old model of I.T.

As we started off this book, the current I.T. model was built on a buy, build, and run model based on the premise that I.T. has to be self-sufficient, and remain operational (onsite and in hot or standby datacenters) in the event of a system fault or site failure. The current architecture overemphasizes this model of I.T. infrastructure that ensures every aspect of the architecture is highly reliable, redundant, and over capacity. The current model is likely built on over engineered hardware, with redundant components, replicated appliances, and mirrored servers, and redundant applications designed to keep everything running 24 x 7 x 365.

Every single component has to be made redundant and highly available, however when you think about it, all you're looking for is the application to remain highly available. Business people don't say they want the application to have synchronous replicated databases, RAID-10 storage, fiber channel connected pipes, and meshed network redundancy. The business people in the organization simply say they want the application to always be available, period. If we start with THAT premise of application continuity, and move away from the thinking of the bits, bytes, hardware, features, and functions, if there's a better way of achieving application continuity, then THAT becomes the focus for the organization's I.T model and business continuity plans.

The True Cost and Overhead of "Server" Operations

From a costing basis, after lengthy surveys, interviews, and crunching numbers for statistical purposes, it was found that 82% of the infrastructure of an application is setup to simply support the application availability. A mere 18% of the infrastructure resources were directly allocated to running the application itself. To quickly and simply net out the basis for that statistic, an example is that servers are rarely if ever running at near full capacity like 80%-90% utilization. Organizations typically run their servers at 30%-40% runtime utilization, and sometimes down the 5%-10% runtime utilization, so that the server has the capacity to meet demand without the organization needing to constantly go out and buy new hardware.

In addition, on top of those servers running with a LOT of capacity headroom, organizations also typically have 2 or 3 redundant servers in a cluster, array, or load balanced model where demand is distributed across multiple systems, thus minimize a central point of failure for all components of the system. The current I.T model of running an application has more than three-quarter of the infrastructure allocated as spare or standby resources, rather than actually being used.

The Total Cost of Running a Server-based I.T. Environment

In addition to the server, storage, and networking environment needed to simply run the application, the application and datacenter environment then has all of the redundancy mentioned in the previous two chapters which raises the overhead to 99% of the overall cost to run the application.

That 99% overhead includes all of the tape backup servers, patching and application management servers, security analysis servers, replicated storage systems, mirrored datacenter environments, etc.

Think about that statistics for a moment. For every 1% of application runtime capacity exists to deliver the functionality of an application, 99% overhead exists to keep the application redundant, highly available, backed up, updated, and managed. The I.T. operational inefficiencies are easily calculated and then leveraged in an ROI-comparison between running an application on-premise in a current I.T. operational model, and moving the application to a modern shared cloud I.T operational model.

The Case Study of Email as a Service

Email as a Service has been a very successful model already broadly in use by hundreds of thousands of enterprises around the world, and is commonly cited as a case study for the benefits and justification for cloud-based applications. While early environments of Microsoft's Business Productivity Online Service (BPOS) struggled in reliability and feature/functionality, roll forward 5 years and Office 365 has proven to be feature rich, highly reliable, and extremely secure.

Email is frequently identified as one of the most important communication applications in an enterprise. Most organizations state that downtime to email can completely halt all communications in the organization, and that email needs to "just work". However, beyond simply working, because email is the backbone of organizations for communications within the organization, and external to the organization. Organizations typically over architect their email systems with 2-3 times as many servers than are needed, 2-3 times the storage (in terabytes and hundreds of terabytes) than is needed, and redundancy upon redundancy upon redundancy from everything from hard drive systems, to frontend server redundancy, to backend server redundancy, to directory look-up and authentication processes, and so on.

For organizations that have shifted their email system to something like Office 365, the organizations now have the most current version of the Microsoft Exchange email system, they get email archiving and retention, they get modern mobile device access, the latest in anti-spam and anti-virus tools, a full eDiscovery and Legal Hold tool, and at an operational cost that,

21

when assessed and truly compared to current email system expenses, turns out to be at a significantly lower cost point.

With organizations having shifted to a cloud-hosted email system, the internal personnel that used to be dedicated to managing and maintaining the email system are now available to spend more time on more important security focused tasks, true frontend business operations tasks, and working to ensure that the new modernized applications are optimized and meeting the business goals and objectives of the organization.

The Case Study of Websites as a Services

Websites as a Service is also a great case study on the benefits an organization receives as part of the process of modernizing applications. For websites, whether it's the organization's www public site, its intranet site, or the frontend of a business application, the actual running of a webserver requires very minimal resources. Many organizations have a server dedicated to hosting a Web application, which might be running on Java, Microsoft .NET Framework, or the like. However, in addition to the server running the basic Web application, the organization likely has 2, 3, or more redundant servers load balanced and replicated so that if the Web application server fails, there's another server available to take up the load.

This redundancy exists full time so that no user is inconvenienced in the event of a failure. However, the redundancy comes at a big cost for the organization since a Web application that requires less than 5% utilization of a system, which is then made 3x redundant now has only 5% application demand against 300% available resources.

Web applications are frequently the target of conversion to a Platform as a Service (PaaS) model. PaaS moves the native application code to the cloud, and the application no longer has multiple systems effectively doing nothing. All of that redundancy is now abstracted within the cloud and does not need to be maintained by the organizations I.T., in effect efficiently outsourcing the redundant infrastructure. The focus is on providing the required capacity to the users for the running of the Web content, not on all of the capacity allocated to non-essential services directed specifically at the application. PaaS is covered in more detail in Chapter 6 of this book.

5 APPLICATION MODERNIZATION

Up until now, we have setup the groundwork for the basis of modernizing our environment, rather than simply putting our heads down and upgrading applications to the latest on-premise version or migrating everything to the cloud. In this chapter, we'll further develop the strategy and structure of modernizing applications, with a focus on best practices around decision making on the shift of updating applications in a manner that makes most sense.

Replacing Server Focused with Application Focused Services

The key to application modernization is to update the thinking that an application equates to a brand or a server or a system. Instead of thinking that a Web application requires Microsoft Internet Information Server (IIS), or a financial system requires Oracle, instead focus on the business side of the application.

It's replacing a server focused view of applications with a user perspective view of what they do or need to do in their job. The financial analyst thinks of transactional calculations and financial modeling as their job and task, they don't call themselves a Microsoft Excel specialist. Or the accounting manager focuses on double entry accounting tasks, payables, and receivables, and does not describe their trade expertise as an Oracle Financials specialist. They are concerned with the business processes and not the technologies.

While initially users are concerned whether they can do their job with a different tool, it's amazing how responsive users are when they get a better tool, and a better solution, that ultimately makes the execution of their job easier and better. Even in cases where the employee ends up doing the same thing in a different tool with no improvement in features or functions that help the employee do more, it might be that the underlying application is easier or more cost effective for the organization to host, manage, and upgrade on an ongoing basis. In that case, the benefit is in doing the exact same thing, but with a tool that makes better sense for the organization.

A couple good analogies are found in decisions buyers make when they purchase a new car. Sometimes a new car has significant benefits over the old car, like a shift from a 2-door sedan to a 5-passenger sport utility vehicle (SUV). While the old vehicle was great for the young couple, now with 2 kids, trying to get the car seat and kids into the back seat of the 2-door sedan is difficult. The SUV is nothing more than a vehicle that transports everyone from one place to another, it likely doesn't change how fast the family gets to and from school, or the market, or the parents to work. However, the extra door, extra backseat space, extra trunk space makes it easier for the family to use the vehicle, so the transition to the SUV has tangible improvements for the family.

In contrast, in another analogy, a couple with no kids that replaced an old 2-door sedan with a new 2-door sedan may have gotten a new vehicle with no real feature improvements. But the key difference is the new vehicle just "runs better." Compared to their old sedan that required constant maintenance at night to ensure it would start in the morning, the new vehicle itself hasn't added any new features as perceived by the primary driver but it did provide a significant improvement in eliminating the need for constant servicing that the old vehicle required to keep it running.

This is the same modernization experience that applications will go through in an organization. There will be times when the shift to a new application may add significant improvements in features and functions, and other times there may be changes to something new, with little or no perceived benefits to the application owner and user, but will have significant improvements on the "backend" in what it takes to keep the application running every day.

"Modernization" may mean improving the application with new and better functionality, or modernization may mean a change that reduces the unseen costs of maintaining and managing problem some system on the backend.

Software as a Service for Commodity-based Applications

There are many applications that are critical to the day-to-day success of the organization which have been cloud-based solutions for many years. Many times personnel would say they don't "trust" the cloud because of security or reliability concerns, and how some application like email or their line of business application is so critical that they couldn't trust someone else running or managing it. But then, when asked what payroll service the organization uses, it turns out that every employee paycheck is electronically processed, payroll directly deposited to employee's accounts, and employee access their payroll information via a Web browser to a cloud-based payroll system, which is a SaaS application. The same organization that says they don't trust an outsourced cloud service for a critical secure business application, is the same one that in reality uses an outsourced cloud-based solution (also a SaaS application) to pay employees every month.

Or an organization that ships their products to their customers that uses a Web-based package scheduling and tracking system, that organization is also already utilizing a SaaS cloud solution to get their goods to their clients. Bill of ladings are processed electronically over the Internet, the scheduling for pick-up is Web-based, and the search for the tracking status is also done via an application or Web-app.

Cloud or Internet based SaaS applications doesn't mean the organization has decreased the reliability, performance, or quality of service. The key is to ensure the provider of the service has the right systems in place to ensure uptime, performance, and ongoing maintenance and modernization of their application as a service.

This Software as a Service (SaaS) model has proven to be an extremely valuable service for many core business applications. As already identified, tasks such as payroll services, package shipping and delivery services, and application services such as electronic mail, client relationship management, and file collaboration have been core applications that have lent themselves as commodity systems similar across many industries, that have proven to be prime examples of successful Software as a Service application models.

Email as a Service (Office 365 / Google Mail)

Electronic mail as a service has been cited time and time again as a key business application for organizations, and it is effectively one of the most broadly used applications as a service. As much as many organizations will claim that their email is one of the most critical business communications applications they own and must remain internally managed and serviced to ensure the level of security and integrity, at the end of the day, email is the same across various industries, business sizes, and business focus. A person in a 10-employee organization sends and receives email the exact same way a person in a 10,000-employee organization does. Users type a message, maybe attach a file to the message, and click to send the message. Email users around the world receive emails regardless of their line of business the exact same way where they select to open a message, they read the message, then they delete or save the message.

The key thing organizations want to ensure is that the email system is always working, and that their employee's messages retain a high level of security and privacy. But just like the cloud and internet-based payroll system, there's not many organizations that would say that payroll isn't highly secure nor something that is okay if employee paychecks are late because of a reliability problem by the payroll service. Hosted providers that are serious about email reliability and security understand the importance of their role, can build their system and services to provide that level of protections, and run their operations as well if not better than what an organization can internally do themselves.

The key players in the cloud-based hosted email business are Microsoft with their Office 365 service, and Google with their Gmail for Business service. These organizations are two of the largest and most well-funded organizations in the world. Each organization has spent billions of dollars and invested years in the development, management, and maintenance of their cloud-hosted email systems. They clearly understand if they fail their customers, they will not survive in the hosted email sector for long, and thus maintain an extremely high rigor in security and reliability of their services.

And because Microsoft and Google serve millions of users worldwide across virtually every industry, their attention to the needs of this diverse population of users across language support, device support, operating system support, end user support, and the like is of the caliber of a global enterprise grade solution.

These providers are constantly improving the features and functions of their service to retain existing customers, and to attract new customers looking for a top notch solution. And while each organization has had bumps in the performance or reliability of their service early on in the offering of their service, as time has gone on, these key providers of email as a service have matured and improved their offerings to achieve enterprise quality, security, and support expected of a reliable and dependent service provider.

As such, email as a service has grown as a core hosted service offering with tens of millions if not hundreds of millions of users relying on the hosted services of key email as a service provided service.

CRM as a Service (Salesforce.com)

Another common, almost defacto provider of a service is Salesforce.com and what they provide as client relationship management or enterprise relationship management as a service. Unlike email as a service that gained popularity because of the commonality that email in every enterprise is effectively the same across the user of every employee in the organization across various industries, CRM as a service was quite the opposite. CRM is an application that only a handful of employees in an organization use, and in many cases the use of CRM is unique to that business or industry.

For a highly customized application used by a limited number of users, CRM was an expensive application for organizations to setup, maintain, and manage in the enterprise. Salesforce.com took this specialty application, developed a SaaS product, and offered as a monthly subscription service, and created an ecosystem that allowed third party providers to customize the Salesforce application to meet the specific needs of specific users in an industry. By providing a service that an organization can pay for only the number of licenses for the number of users that actually use the service, that can be customized to meet the specific needs of the organization, CRM as a service was transformed early on as a solution that was better off being offered as a hosted service than for organizations to try to build and manage the platform internally.

File System as a Service (Box, DropBox, OneDrive)

Filesystem as a Service by key providers like Box.com, DropBox, or OneDrive evolved and gained popularity for a much different reason than email or CRM as a service. Filesystem services grew out of a need by users to share and collaborate with users internal and external to their organization. Because most I.T. organizations were focused on what was deemed to be more critical business applications like ERP systems or other core line of business applications, basic file sharing and collaboration was not given the same level of attention by I.T. services.

As Box and DropBox grew popularity by students and individuals sharing documents easily over the Internet from any device (Windows, Mac, iPhones, Android devices), these file sharing and collaboration solutions started to be introduced into enterprises without business or I.T. approval or even awareness. By the time I.T. realized that their users had found a "backdoor" application for a key business collaboration and communication task, it was too late to stop it, as a whole model for business information sharing was by then too engrained in the day-to-day tasks and processes of employees.

The users of file system as a service validated the business need for a simple solution to share content among employees and between organizations. The effort for many organizations has been to bring this functionality into a company owned and managed solution that fits within the security policies and practices of the organization, and eliminate hundreds of unmanaged individual accounts being used throughout the enterprise.

And with file sharing and collaboration functionality bundled into application suites, organizations are already paying for file sharing services as part of their email solutions, so a shift from a 3rd party solution to an integrated solution has been the focus of enterprises. To address the concerns of security, document permissions, and data leakage, I.T. organizations are focusing their time on implementing and enforcing electronically stored information policies for the management of business owned data.

This shift of I.T. resources from building and running file storage and management systems, to having the I.T. resources focused on policy development and enforcement is the change that comes about with the transition to modern application and datacenter services. More time is available for I.T. personnel to rightly focus on areas of business importance, rather than on basic hardware and software installation and maintenance.

Choosing Functionality over Product Brand

Cloud services can be setup, enabled, and used almost immediately, which accelerates an organizations adoption of cloud-based solutions. In the old days, organizations had to be careful choosing an application because of the significant investment in hardware and software along with months of setting up the infrastructure needed to even start to play with the software. The decision to choose a cloud service is more based on the functionality the solution provides than simply the product brand. Cloud providers are very awareness of the "stickiness" or lack of "stickiness" of their products. When email is email, and file sharing is file sharing, the differentiation from one brand to another is based on customer satisfaction of the solution. As easy as it was for the organization to originally spin up a cloud-based solution, the organization can now quickly shift over to a different solution in the same time and effort it has historically taken an organization to do a version level upgrade of an on-premise product.

So the decision making of an organization on what product to select is heavily dependent on the features and functions the users will get from the service. However, that said, cloud services over the past 3-4 years have proven that the key leader in a solution can quickly fall from favor if the cloud service provider doesn't continue to invest in the development of their solution. Many cloud-based solutions are developed and run by organizations that have never shown a profit in the running of their operations. The key for any business to stay in business long term is to offer up a solution and run a business that can sustain itself. With the focus on acquisition by many cloud providers, rather than the development of a business model based on sustainability of the organization, the selection of the cloud based solution, regardless of the features and function, still has to be based on an assurance that the organization will remain in business and has a track record of providing improved functionality over time.

Running On-Premise for a Period of Time

As has been noted previously in this book, application modernization doesn't mean that everything needs to be migrated to the cloud, or at least immediately migrated to the cloud. Application modernization has in many cases been focused on assessing the right solution for the organization for each individual application.

For many applications that are extremely custom, for which cloud-based solutions do not exist, or the solution will simply not run at all in the cloud, the effort to move the application to the cloud would be counterproductive. For these applications, deferring the decision on what to do with the application can be put off to a future date. An organization can focus on modernizing other applications and be well under way to getting as much moved to a cloud-based or modern solution based offering, and then circle back to the more difficult solutions for modernization.

APPLICATION MODERNIZATION

6 DATACENTER MODERNIZATION

The previous chapter was on Application Modernization, effectively focusing on the migration of legacy applications to a modern application. This chapter on Datacenter Modernization extends the application modernization concept, and effectively encompasses "everything else" an organization has running in their datacenters.

Getting to the Rest of I.T.

Usually in the Application and Datacenter modernization process, organizations start with transition efforts around migrating email to the cloud, or implementing dev and test scenarios in a cloud-based solution, or replacing legacy applications with specialized SaaS based services. The "rest of I.T." in the transition process takes a holistic approach to all applications and services run by the organization.

The other services may include user identity and authentication, it usually includes backup and business continuity solutions, and it includes management systems. The reason these other services are specifically called out is that, as organizations shift from a datacenter model to a distributed cloud-based model, monitoring systems isn't as simple as loading an agent on all of the servers in a datacenter and monitoring the systems. In the new cloud based model, it may require doing application state monitoring across a number of different cloud-based IaaS, PaaS, and SaaS environments and in some hybrid cases an on-premise environment.

Patch and update management systems in an environment based on cloud services may no longer be needed, as SaaS-based applications typically have no tenant level patching and updating responsibilities. Even for the handful of systems that are left in the datacenter, or the handful of systems that are running as IaaS virtual machines in a cloud environment, the organization has to think whether an enterprise scale server management tool is needed anymore. It was fine have an enterprise grade management system when the organization had 50, 500, 5000 systems to manage, but when the organization is left with a fraction of the number of systems, a simpler solution for management might be to use a basic Windows Update platform, or even a manual process that takes someone in I.T. a couple hours a month to initiate and manage may be more efficient than having a team of people monitoring and managing the management system each day and week.

So the process of modernizing "everything else" in the datacenter may very likely be selectively choosing systems to eliminate and not need any plans for replacement.

Leveraging Identity as a Service

One of the core services that typically remains in the on-premise datacenter toward the very end of the modernization is the organization's identity system. Most organizations rely on Microsoft's Active Directory as the basis for user identity. Almost inevitably, the Active Directory has connectors that link Active Directory on-premise to cloud services like Office 365, Salesforce.com, Microsoft Azure, and the like. The end solution for identity typically takes one of two forms.

One solution for enterprises is to retain Active Directory on-premise as a key authentication point for users in each site. Active Directory has already been consolidated from a distributed site model to a centralized datacenter model as servers and applications have undergone consolidation to corporate datacenters. In other cases, as applications have distributed out to various cloud points, and datacenters being shutdown, we've seen Active Directory being distributed back down to organization site level.

Another solution for enterprises with respective to identity is to move the identity source to a cloud hosted model. Many organizations depend on Active Directory for some type of authentication mechanism and other configuration or security services, whether that's leveraging Group Policies for configuration and security, Active Directory integration of users, groups, computers, and sites, or even 3rd party two-factor authentication tools integrated with Active directory. These organizations may choose to move Active Directory to an IaaS virtual machine running in a cloud or leverage Azure Active Directory cloud identity.

Microsoft Azure Active Directory is a cloud-based centralized identity solution. This is the directory that Office 365 uses. As users logon to their email and authenticate to Azure Active Directory from their laptops, mobile phones, and tablets, the users may just need a cloud-based authentication point like Azure AD and may not have any legacy Active Directory exist at all.

The key decision points are to determine what applications users need to authenticate to, what services are needed, and from what devices the users are connecting from. Are the users connecting from within a corporate office via a corporate device and thus an on-premise instance of the directory makes the most sense? Or are users primarily logging in from somewhere in the world from an Internet connection, with the user accessing cloud SaaS applications from a mobile phone or tablet. In those cases, the user is likely not interacting with a server sitting in a company on-premise site, and would be better served by authenticating to a cloud-based directory.

Many services and functionality can be provided, and some thinking should take place to modernize authentication to applications in a manner that better suits the day to day usage by employees.

Transitioning the Rest of the Datacenter Isn't a One for One Process

Another interesting lesson learned in transitions out of a traditional datacenter model to a modern cloud model is the benefit that consolidation plays in the transition process. Rather than taking 100 servers and migrating the servers to 100 cloud-based servers, the I.T. organization needs to assess a model where consolidation can reduce the footprint of the enterprise.

While the organization may have 100 servers, through consolidation of services such as adding multiple database instances to a single database server, or consolidating multiple web instances to a single (or handful) of servers can decrease the sheer number of systems that'll reside in the I.T. environment down the line.

Many times application servers were built to host a specific application without consideration that the application could co-run on an existing system. During the initial implementation process, application owners are typically target focused on the deployment of their application, not on datacenter optimization. So a simple process of stepping back, identifying applications, and then consolidating applications to fewer systems will help maximize the efficiency of I.T. in the organization, and best optimize the environment as part of the modernization process.

Other applications were built to run in distributed datacenters to be "closer to users," however in this day and age of high speed wide area network connectivity and latency insensitive communication protocols, applications can be centralized without the need to put a server in each and every site. As an example, a content sharing system may have been implemented in 6 site datacenters of the organization, distributing the application infrastructure and enabling close access to localized data for each organizational site. However, in a modernization effort where the application is consolidated to a cloud-based environment, potentially just 1 or 2 distributed cloud-based instances of the application is now needed, thus eliminating the need for a lot of redundant infrastructure. Just as the organization in years prior assessed on performance and redundancy, a new assessment can be conducted to determine if the high speed connectivity options available today will be sufficient to consolidate the application across a single region instead of six.

These are all of the tasks that need to be considered as part of the completion of datacenter modernization. Not simply taking each application and moving them one-to-one into a similarly configured hosted environment, but instead conducting a thorough into a more appropriate modern model that still meets the core needs of the organization.

Simplicity of IaaS

During the datacenter modernization process, many organizations simply capture the running state of an on-premise virtual machine (VM), and import the virtual machine into a cloud-based running VM. This Infrastructure as a Service (IaaS) model most certainly is a relatively easy model of transition and quite frankly is typically the initial step that most organizations take in their journey to the cloud. However, if there's a SaaS application available that does the same thing, or a consolidation model that allows the organization to decrease the number of virtual machines as part of the consolidation and transition process, then the one-for-one migration of systems to IaaS is not the best long term model.

As identified in Chapters 2 and 3 of this book, the challenges with existing I.T. models are all of the operating system, application, patching, updating, monitoring, and system management required to run a "server". By simply moving the server to an IaaS cloud instance of the server, the organization still has the same legacy overhead to manage and maintain. So IaaS really is recommended solely for the simplicity of moving an on-premise instance to a similarly configured cloud instance. However, if the organization can transform the application to a modern SaaS or PaaS model, the organization can eliminate a layer (or two, or three) of ongoing management and maintenance.

Where PaaS Fits In for Datacenter Modernization

Platform as a Service (PaaS) has proven to be a good model for many custom applications. PaaS fits between the removal of all of the overhead of an IaaS virtual machine system, and the limitations that might exist with a SaaS model, for example when the application doesn't exist as a SaaS offering. A good example of PaaS based applications is the running of Websites and Databases in PaaS offerings.

Many of the applications that run in a datacenter, outside of structured email, file sharing, accounting, and ERP systems, are Websites and Databases. In a traditional I.T. model, a Website is a simple HTML, .NET, Java, or other simplified application running on a Web engine like Microsoft's IIS or Apache Web servers. Underlying those Web engine is an operating system (Windows or Linux) and typically a Hypervisor (like VMware or HyperV). The Web Engine, operating system, and hypervisor serve absolutely no operational value or benefit for the running of the Web application, and there's a lot of overhead to patch, manage, backup, and maintain a very thin Web application.

A Web-based PaaS platform allows an organization to simply upload the Web application code to the cloud and run the application. The application owner has to do nothing with the underlying infrastructure running the application. The elimination of server layers greatly decrease the administration and management overhead for the organization.

PaaS still allows the organization to completely customize their Web instance, so whatever colors, form, style that the organization desires is coded in HTML, .NET, Java, or the like. The organization can pay the PaaS hoster to backup the code, replicate the code to another geo region, and add code capacity to increase performance.

And the other common PaaS platform model is the implementation of SQL databases as a PaaS service. A SQL application typically requires a SQL server running on a Windows server running on a Hypervisor. Again, the SQL server, Windows Server, and Hypervisor add no value to the running of the SQL tables and queries other than the underlying infrastructure.

As a PaaS instance of SQL, an organization can upload data, structure it in tables, build cubes, generate reports, secure fields, and address raw SQL queries just as if the query was going to a full SQL server, but without all of the management overhead that would be needed with a full blown virtual machine running a SQL server.

From a costing perspective, SQL as a PaaS offering is a fraction of the cost of building a SQL Server running on Windows because SQL as PaaS is paid for based on real capacity allocation variable on demand, than the building of a fixed configuration IaaS VM with a fixed 16 cores and 256gb of memory that the organization pays for by the number of cores 24 x 7 x 365 whether the application needs that capacity or not.

Cloud capacity can be added and decreased at any time, unlike hardware in a datacenter that had to be budgeted, purchased, acquired, stacked in a rack, configured, installed, and setup 2, 3, or 6 months in advance of needing the capacity. The complete rethinking of the ease and availability of acquiring cloud capacity changes how organizations buy, configure, and run cloud services very differently than the organization has addressed capacity on-premise for the past couple decades.

7 STRATEGY PLANNING FOR APP AND DATACENTER MODERNIZATION

The modernization process for applications and datacenters is a methodical process that takes an organization from their existing state, to the next generation of their I.T. operations. As much as the transition plan deals with technology, it is also a strategic plan that optimizes employee productivity with technical solutions that meet the needs of the employee's tasks.

Developing a Methodical Process for an Optimized Transition

The modernization process is unlike historical I.T. architecture and budgeting processes that have traditionally focused on taking existing systems, and upgrading them to the latest release of the same system with minor updates to leverage new features and functions. This modernization process, when done right, looks to assess what employees do, and match an appropriate technical solution to meet the tasks of the employees.

The strategic planning process is a gap analysis exercise that determines the right tools and solutions based on employee requirements, and then a technology transition process to shift from the existing platform of technical solutions to the modern solution.

Inventorying Current Applications

The first step in the process to an optimized datacenter with modernized applications is to inventory existing applications to understand what currently exists in the environment. The exercise is to categorize applications based on what they are and who uses them. An example might be:

Microsoft Exchange	Email and Calendaring	Everyone
Salesforce.com	CRM	Sales
Oracle Financials	General Accounting	Accounting
System Center	Monitoring and Mgmt	I.T.
Intranet	Old Intranet	Not Used

At this point, the inventory assessment is merely to ensure later on that application functionality is addressed either in upgraded versions of applications, or in application replacement tasks. Additionally, the current inventory will help in the retirement of applications over time. Far too often, organizations move forward in their modernization process, but never eliminate the older legacy applications. This inventory list will be used to check off applications as the organization moves forward.

Assessing Employee Tasks and Technology Usage

The next step in the modernization process is a very critical step that involves assessing what employees in the organization do, and how the existing applications they use are leveraged as part of the day to day of the employees job responsibilities. What is helpful to understand in the process is whether their existing applications are useful in what they do, or if there are things they would like to do that they cannot do today. With a "wishlist" mapped out, as the application modernization is conducted, the suitability of an application can be determined.

Application replacement may not be part of the scope of the modernization effort. I.T. also may not necessarily find a replacement application that includes ALL of the items on employee's wishlist. However, if an application is not used by employees, or the application is completely unusable by employees, the assessment could be used to determine whether an application could potentially be eliminated or really needs to be replaced as part of the modernization process.

Some organizations may spend less than a week doing an employee application usage assessment, others might spend 2-3 months. Any insight the I.T. organization can gain from better understanding the tasks and responsibilities of employees and how current applications are leveraged can assist in the modernization process. This understanding provides a clearer path for application upgrade, replacement, or elimination can help the organization modernize their application and datacenter operations.

Preparing an Initial Gap Analysis

With an inventory list of applications in use by employees, along with a list of needs and application suitability assessment, the next step is to develop a gap analysis of application effectiveness. The gap analysis should net out:

- Applications that Work As Is
- Applications that May Require Further Review
- Applications that Aren't Used at All

Clearly, applications that aren't used at all should be flagged for elimination. This may include applications that are marginally used where the functionality could be replaced by other applications so that the transition process includes moving users off of underutilized applications.

Applications that meet the general needs of users will be flagged as applications that will be transitioned in some form or another. Whether the application will be upgraded to a new version, hosted on-premise, or moved to the cloud solution will be addressed in the next step. For now, just a general flag that the application will survive and be addressed upcoming.

The applications that are flagged for further review may not necessarily be replaced, but in the next step in determining modernization, a review of the application and suitability of a replacement should be conducted. This application gap analysis provides visibility into what applications may be replaced or updated to truly meet the business needs of the organization. A roadmap can be created to identify the timing of which applications will be retained, which applications will be upgraded on-premise, which applications will be migrated to the cloud, and which applications need to be replaced as part of the application modernization process. The previous table can be extended with additional columns such as:

Microsoft Exchange	Works Fine as is	Mobile Support Desired
Salesforce.com	Works Fine as is	No Changes Needed
Oracle Financials	Works Fine as is	Over 5-yrs old, Upgrade
System Center	Works Fine as is	Cloud Version available?
Intranet	Not Used Anymore	Eliminate

Identifying More Effective Apps and Services for Employees

With an inventory of applications and an initial assessment of which applications will be replaced, retained, or eliminated, the next step is to determine the transition state of the application. Additional columns of the initial application table can be created to identify a timeline and proposed disposition of each application in use in the environment.

The table could be extended with the following:

Microsoft Exchange	Replace with Office 365	Within Next 6-mo
Salesforce.com	No Changes Needed	No Changes
Oracle Financials	Keep On-prem for Now	Upgrade Version
System Center	Evaluate OMS/Intune	Go Cloud 1-2 Yrs
Intranet	Power Off for 30-days	Eliminate thereafter

The additional columns of the table will identify a projected timeline when applications will be upgraded, updated, transitioned, or eliminated. This will also build out the framework of a transition roadmap and can be the basis for budgeting and a timeline for the modernization initiative.

Building a Transition Plan

The basis for the transition plan have been outlined in the steps building up of the planning table. The table can be sorted to note an initial assessment on timing with budget numbers added to the table for costing as well as a "complexity" rating along with an "impact" rating and a priority rating for each line item.

The table builds the basis of the transition plan that can be sorted and executed based on complexity, priority, and impact. Some items may need to be upgraded sooner than later due to supportability of the current application. Rather than upgrading to a current version of the application, the organization can consider upgrading off an old or obsolete version of an application into a version that might be SaaS-based or cloud-hosted. Additionally, the upgrade process can address more than just a version update but could also include enhancements in features and functions.

Aside from transitioning based on obsolescence, some applications may be targeted for transition because of the current cost or current (lack of) security of the application. These factors can drive priority of the transition to eliminate a pending license renewal cost or ongoing support contract cost of the application, or address a concern the organization has where the application lacks enterprise security, data leakage, and data integrity controls that are expected of all applications in the enterprise.

Organizations typically upgrade applications every 3-5 years, and so the cost and effort to upgrade applications from one version to another can be reallocated to the cost of transitioning the application from the current version to a newer, more modern version of the application or similar application. This modernizes the environment by moving the application off of an on-premise model to a potentially more efficient and effective cloud-hosted applications.

8 BUDGETING FOR MODERNIZATION

One of the exercises commonly associated with an application and datacenter modernization initiative is the budgeting cost of the effort. Not just of the one-time cost to perform migrations, but also the ongoing cost of any licensing or subscriptions necessary to run the application. This chapter covers the common budgeting components calculated during a modernization initiative.

Assessing Transition Costs Relative to Traditional Version Migration Costs

One of the key costing factors calculated in the modernization process is the transition cost from the current operating environment to the new operating environment. As an example, if the organization is shifting from

Exchange email on-premise to Office 365 email in the cloud, a cost calculation is assessed on what it will take to complete the migration.

While the cost of the migration certainly needs to be calculated and funded for completion, the cost to migrate to a cloud-based solution is typically the same cost the organization would have incurred if it upgraded from one version to the next version of an application.

Back to the example of the Exchange to Office 365 email migration cost, for organization that have upgraded Exchange email every 3-5 years, the cost to upgrade to a newer version of Exchange on-premise is about the same cost (and effort) to migrate the organization from Exchange on-premise to Office in 365 in the cloud. The process involves a planning process, setting up core migration servers, conducting a prototype and pilot migrations, and then completing the migration with any applicable administration and enduser training.

In transitions to cloud-based applications, there may be initial training costs to familiarize I.T. personnel on the new way of managing and administrating the new solution, or if a solution is replaced with a completely new or different product, then enduser training may need to be budgeted. However, in general, the cost of transitioning to a new version is typically not significantly more expensive to complete than other migrations performed by the enterprise in the past.

Assessing CapEx and OpEx Costs in the New World of I.T.

What does change in the budgeting and costing of modern applications may come in the form of licensing or subscription costing. In older application licensing models, organizations bought a product (hardware and/or software) and at most purchased a maintenance contract for the application or systems.

Under many new licensing models, the cost of the application is paid for as a "monthly cost" on a "per user basis". The more users the organization has, the higher monthly cost of the application. Additionally, the cost is billed typically every month on a perpetual basis for as long as the organization uses the application. Unlike some legacy applications where the organization bought the application outright 10 or 15 years ago and hasn't paid a cent for the application license since, there is an ongoing cost associated with most applications these days. This ongoing cost also typically includes upgrades and support contract arrangements. And cloud-based applications are typically upgraded behind the scenes so that users of the application get an updated version on a rolling update basis instead of interruption every 3-5 years and a massive retraining on ALL of the new things in the application. So the model changes, subscription licensing model changes, yet a much simpler and more predictable model for costing is the result of the modern cloud based application model.

The other change in the new model of licensing and subscriptions is this rolling monthly subscription cost. Rather than a major purchase of hardware, software, and services every 3-5 years that an organization may classify as a Capital Expense (CapEx), the new subscription models typically include hardware, software, and maintenance on a rolling monthly cost basis as a "per user subscription" basis. The costing model shifts to an Operational Expense (OpEx) model. This may (or may not) impact how the organization does their financial planning shifting CapEx expenses to OpEx expenses, something to explore if there is a question or concern on how new model licensing is contracted.

Comparing Overall Costs to Historical Costs of I.T.

As organizations shift from a CapEx to an OpEx costing model, many times it is hard for the organization to justify an OpEx monthly expenditure while the organization is still depreciating hardware and software from a historical CapEx model. The key is to not encumber the CapEx and OpEx expenses to a single application, but rather look to shift CapEx depreciation expense to offset current and future adjusted cost allocations.

As much as an organization may be shifting off of Microsoft Exchange on-premise to Office 365 in the cloud and eliminating the need for 15 or 20 Exchange servers, storage, and other I.T. services, the organization may have budgeted and be looking to purchase more servers, storage, and networking capacity to fulfill on demands of other I.T. initiatives.

Instead of buying more Capital expensed hardware and software, the organization can repurpose unused Exchange servers and storage, to the part of the business that was planning on purchasing more servers and storage. This reallocation of costs helps the organization spread out CapEx expenses over a 2-3 year period, and can eliminate any near term impact to the financials of the organization in this shift from CapEx to OpEx integrated services. This is commonly missed in the budgeting and cost analysis of modernizing I.T., the effective repurposing of encumbered assets. This is also why a well-structured roadmap strategy can take in account a transition process that includes financial and CapEx/OpEx depreciation schedules into the roadmap. Instead of buying more storage or more servers to meet the rolling demands of the organization, the Capital Expense of hardware purchases if properly arranged to coincide with the transition of storage and hardware rich solutions that are moving to the cloud can eliminate the need for the purchase of more Capital expense goods.

Creating an ROI Analysis for the Modern App and Datacenter Environment

Another common practice that I.T. organizations need to consider is how the Return on Investment (ROI) is calculated in the analysis of the modernization of applications and datacenter operations. Specific to the costing of current running systems to a comparable cloud-running system, organizations mistakenly cost a one-for-one analysis. If the organization currently has 8 servers running 16-core and 256gb of RAM each, the organization frequently costs the exact same quantity and configuration in the cloud. The cost of the cloud at that capacity is very expense, and the ROI doesn't make sense.

However, as covered in Chapter 6, the cloud modernization model is not a one-for-one target of all servers and systems. When organizations had to plan and budget hardware purchases 6-12 months in advance, and hardware took 2-4 months to acquire, setup, configure, and make the resource available, organizations over-purchased hardware to meet virtually any demand the organization may need in capacity planning. And when the I.T. organization also had to build in high availability and disaster recovery planning capacity, then the over allocation of hardware was now double and triple allocated.

But in a cloud model where additional capacity can be spun up in 5-10 minutes as well as cloud capacity can be reduced in just a few minutes as well, an organization can buy and implement capacity closer to what they really need and use. Additionally, when Service Level Agreements on cloud runtime and disaster recovery is part of the cost of the hosted service, the organization doesn't need to buy 2x or 3x the number of systems when the cloud provider has already included in a component for high availability and geo-redundancy.

For the same organization that had 8 high capacity systems with 16-core and 256gb of RAM frequently finds that the organization can run off 2 systems running 4-core and 128gb of RAM with no impact on performance, and with the ability to scale more capacity within 10-minutes. THIS decrease from 8 servers to 2 servers, and the elimination of over 100-core processors can eliminate thousands if not tens of thousands of dollars a month in the costing model, and drastically improve the ROI calculations to metrics that are more applicable to the workload scenarios.

Calculating the True Runtime Needs of the Systems

While the previous section notes that an organization can use a significantly lower capacity of servers and systems, how does the I.T. organization calculate what it really needs? In simple terms, the organization assesses the server utilization and runs calculations off the peak and the sustained runtime calculations.

If a server normally runs at 6% utilization and peaks at 10% utilization, then an optimized configuration would be 10-15 times fewer server resources than currently configured. Memory is sometimes harder to calculate as many applications these days use up all of the memory available, so even if an application only really needs 32gb of memory, if the system has 128gb of memory, the application will load up and use all 128gb of memory for cache whether it really uses it or not. The configuration of "dynamic memory" for many systems has the application optimized for the actual memory used to operate the application on a runtime basis.

Relying on manufacturer specifications or recommended configurations when the manufacturer is still basing its specifications on an older traditional inhouse server model is usually not a good metric to work from either. Some vendors have modernized their recommended specifications to address this change in resource allocation, and truly provides specs that are more application to the dynamic hosted cloud datacenter model.

When assessing the requirements for high availability and site recoverability, working with the Service Level Agreements of the hosted environment, as well as evaluating options for operational continuity can provide a better allotment of systems needed for the running of the application. Again, keep in mind that additional systems can be brought online typically within 5-10 minutes, so the focus for the cloud environment shifts from monitoring systems for uptime, versus the new model of monitoring systems for capacity demands, and then automating the process to bring more capacity online as needed.

Summarizing the Business Benefits of the Modern I.T. Environment

As much as this chapter has been focused on costing, budgeting, and calculating ROI, an important factor to include in the calculation model is the business benefit that the Modern I.T. environments provides for the business. Significant business benefits can be achieved by eliminating servers and datacenters, and refocusing of I.T. resources on allocating creative ways to make I.T. a business enabler. Other business benefits include core factors in eliminating unused resources and capacity to a model that is "on demand" where resources can spin up in minutes when needed than constantly running excess capacity.

Other organizations have found the elimination of datacenters and servers as key factors that allow the organization to move from site to site without having to spend months and millions of dollars planning for a costly and time consuming "datacenter move". Without racks and racks of servers taking up expensive lease hold space, or the special electrical power, cooling, and security requirements traditionally allocated to organizations to run on-premise servers and I.T. systems, the organization is nimbler to expand, move, consolidate, or simplify their business site models.

Additional benefits cited by organizations in their modernization of I.T. has been the ability for the organization to concurrently address security and business continuity services. When "servers" are located in a site location that is dependent on complex perimeter security with a focus on protecting the "datacenter" vs applications that by definition are hosted in the cloud or in distributed locations, the security and business continuity is based on the protection of the data itself, not of the designation of the site.

Data protection and security enables the focus of the integrity of the data wherever the content resides, and thus a transition to a distributed cloud-based model inherently demands the integration of data continuity and security protections, and site and datacenter integrity and security. This greatly improves an organization's ability to have users access information from anywhere on any device since the data in transit and distribution has to be included in the plan, than by depending solely on firewalls and site security as the method of protection (which doesn't work when users access the content outside of the site and datacenter). This forces the organization to provide more modern security controls closer to the actual data, rather than just relying on the perimeter security controls.

There are a number of these benefits that come as part of the benefits in modernizing I.T. that extend far beyond simply doing a cost analysis of the migration cost and the monthly subscription cost that is commonly associated with a cost/benefit analysis.

9 RETHINKING MONITORING AND MANAGEMENT SERVICES

As enterprises modernize their applications and datacenters, one of the benefits that result from the effort is the shift in how I.T. systems are monitored and managed. The shift in these operational services simplifies process and decreases costs when the modernization process nears completion.

The Evolution of I.T. Management in the Modern App and Datacenter Environment

Traditional I.T. management systems are based on monolithic systems that are built on monitoring and managing a datacenter full of applications, servers, and systems. I.T. management systems include monitoring the uptime of various servers, patching and updating the systems, and monitoring the security and integrity of systems.

However, as organizations shift from running "systems" to utilizing hosted servers, monitoring the running of a SaaS-based application simplifies down to just monitoring that the hosted environment is up and available. The underlying infrastructure of the hosted application is not the responsibility of the tenant user. The shift turns to application monitoring instead of server and system monitoring. Additionally, since the organization is buying the service and not hosting and managing their own systems and servers, there is no underlying systems to patch and update. The organization still needs to monitor and manage the networking infrastructure, network connections, and Internet connections as well as endpoint client systems, however the scope of responsibility for the organization is a fraction of what it used to be when the I.T. organization was responsible for managing and maintaining complete datacenters full of servers, storage systems, and application servers.

Another shift in management of a modernized application and datacenter environment is the amount of importance placed on a "site". When a site included the core datacenter that required all servers and systems to be operational for site employees as well as employees in other sites to be able to access key business systems, then the uptime of that site was critical. Entire failover datacenters have been created to ensure redundancy not only the event of an application server failure, but in a catastrophic site failure.

But if a site holds no servers or systems, or a limited number of application servers and systems, and the key applications are hosted outside of the operational site, a site failure has limited impact on the business continuity of the organization. With employees using mobile phones, tablets, and laptop computers connected to the Internet on a day to day basis has their primary site fail due to a power outage, regional disaster, or the like, the employee can work from home, from a different site, or potentially any place with an Internet connection.

Expensive power generators, redundant networking equipment, redundant Internet connections, and the like could be eliminated if the business continuity plan of the organization is to simply have employees go home and work remotely. This provides organizations significant flexibility in how it plans its business continuity strategy, and how site mobility completely changes core cost factors in business operations.

Reassessing the Need for Patch and Update Management

As has been identified and described previously, without an extensive set of servers and systems to patch and update, organizations that have shifted core business services to cloud-based solutions changes the nature of how the organization has addressed patch and update management. In a

SaaS application model, there are no servers for the organization to patch and update. Entire infrastructures have been built in the past to simply manage and maintain servers and application systems.

This is also why a movement away from IaaS should be part of an organization's modernization plan. If the organization simply bundled up all on-premise virtual machines and forklifted the VMs to a cloud-hosted IaaS model, the organization still has ALL of the same monitoring, patching, and updating responsibilities up in the cloud as it had before on-premise. The organization hasn't made drastic improvements in minimizing their I.T. responsibilities.

Granted there will be applications that the organization will need to maintain as fully operational virtual machines that will need to be patched and updated. However, if the quantity is 80%, 70%, even 50% of what the datacenter used to look like, it's that much fewer systems to patch, manage, and update on a regular basis.

And if an organization is able to get the number of servers to manage and maintain down to just a handful, a full blown enterprise patching and management system may not be required, and definitely not one with an expensive distribution of servers and complexity that was once needed to manage 5x or 10x as many systems in the past.

Managing the management system has become costly for organizations, and a staged approach to minimize and potentially eliminate systems that require an extensive management overhead greatly benefits the overall cost of maintaining I.T.'s cost for operations.

Evaluating Monitoring and Management "As a Service"

Just as business applications have shifted to an "as a Service" model for email, file sharing, document collaboration, CRM, accounting, and the like, monitoring and management systems can be purchased "as a Service" as well. Cloud-based monitoring solutions can be leveraged to monitor cloud-services or on-premise server systems, with runtime and health dashboards providing critical informational data.

Cloud-based patch management and update solutions are also available to be purchased on a per server, per month basis that can be leveraged to keep the limited number of systems still requiring ongoing updates to be maintained.

Security monitoring and threat analytics solutions are available "as a Service" to create a holistic view of the security footprint of the enterprise for not only cloud-based solutions, but also for servers and systems still residing within an organization's datacenter.

All of these systems can eliminate the need for enterprise hosted, configured, and managed systems that ultimately remove the management systems out of the enterprise datacenters for ongoing maintenance and support.

Handling Downtime and System Faults in a Modern Environment

As has been described earlier in this chapter, business continuity is no longer the sole responsibility of each organization's I.T. department to create redundancy and disaster recovery plans. SaaS-based applications typically have published Service Level Agreements. Beyond the published Service Level Agreement, a review of historical data can validate whether the service provider has met the published SLA, exceeded the published SLA, and specifically where problems have occurred in the past.

There is the possibility of an organization extending the SLA of their SaaS provider with their own redundancy or even third party redundancy solutions, however rather than simply buying or building a redundant set of systems or services to build what is believed to be a more resilient environment, an assessment on the cause of previous failures and the impact of what it means to switchover to a resilient environment needs to be reviewed.

Many times the interruption caused by "failing over" to a resilient environment and then "failing back" can be more disruptive than the time of the outage itself. Other assessments of the cause of an outage may be caused by other infrastructure failures such as an electronical power failure in a site that causes outage. As much as the organization may have purchased the ability to failover their SaaS-based solution to some redundant solution, if the power is out at the Corporate office, the actual application failover will have no impact on addressing the power failure at the Corporate site. Employees could just leave the business office, go home or go to some place that has power, and fire up their laptop or smartphone and gain access to their applications.

The whole nature of business continuity has changed with the transition to a modernized application and datacenter model. If the potential downtime of an application is 2-hours a year, the organization has to really think whether it will get value from spending $100,000, $250,000, or $1-million a year to protect against downtime. This cost/benefit analysis has proven to be even more limiting when "someone" has to make the call whether to failover to a redundant system with the interruption that can cause, or just wait out the outage. Even in traditional standby datacenter models where someone has to "pull the trigger" to failover the organization, it could be hours before someone finally decides to cutover the organization to the standby datacenter only to have the primary datacenter come online minutes after the switchover decision and now the organization has a very costly "failback" scenario to deal with.

Addressing Security in a Broadly Distributed I.T. Model

The strategy for enterprise security also changes in a modernized I.T. model. Unlike I.T. of the past, where all servers and systems were in a single site or datacenter where organizations would put up firewalls and intrusion detection devices, in a distributed I.T. model that includes SaaS providers, putting a firewall around all application points is not feasible and not a productive effort.

The focus in a distributed model that includes SaaS-based applications is to identify users and to protect critical data. User identification is important to clearly know that a user logging on and accessing information is truly the person that the organization assumes is accessing the system. This might include some form of multi-factor authentication that validates a user identity. This also includes role based security as well as content classification that clearly identifies who should access what information.

As organizations focuses on content security instead of site security, the ability for the organization to manage and implement security is actually easier and better than traditional site security. Site security has proven to have drastic limitations as data is accessed by mobile users, or stored in various cloud-hosted and SaaS-based models. However, with security associated to content, applied by policies through classification, and associated by roles of individuals, the organization can better control content access in transit and at rest regardless of the target storage device or location.

10 RETRAINING PERSONNEL FOR THE NEW WORLD OF I.T.

The last core chapter of this book focuses on the changing nature of I.T. management and I.T. personnel that will be managing and maintaining this new world of the modern I.T. environment.

The Decline of the Buy, Build, and Run Model

With the better part of three decades of I.T. experience in buying, building, and running I.T., changing to a new model has been, is, and will be a challenge for I.T. organizations. It takes a complete new rethinking of the of I.T. to embrace the fact that I.T. is different these days, which requires a change in management and support models.

I.T. organizations no longer spend weeks or months buying and building hardware systems. Entire groups of I.T. personnel are no longer needed to rack and stack equipment, and watch blinking lights to make sure hardware systems are running. Processes like replacing backup tapes, monitoring system queues, restarting system services, or rebooting servers are no longer the daily tasks of I.T. organizations that have their applications in a SaaS or PaaS based model. Even the ongoing process of planning and performing system maintenance, updates, and upgrades are eliminated from the job responsibilities of I.T. personnel.

This doesn't mean that I.T. employees are out of a job though. As much as many mundane tasks have been eliminated from an organization, the evolution of I.T. in a cloud-optimized environment refocuses the tasks of I.T. personnel to proactive points of responsibilities that benefit the organization in improving security, optimizing employee use, and leveraging data to provide improved business services, and decreasing the cost and overhead typically associated with I.T. operations.

Focusing on Leveraging Functionality of SaaS Model Applications

In organizations that have implemented SaaS-based applications, I.T. personnel now spend their time optimizing the organization's use of SaaS applications. The two major areas include feature and function optimization, and workload optimization.

Within all SaaS applications are a series of features and functions included in the application itself, many of which are disabled by default. Some features and functions are utilized by the users, and some features and functions are managed by the application administrator. In the traditional I.T. environment where so much time was spent simply keeping the system operational and well maintained, most I.T. personnel had little time left over to actually understand how the applications work, or what else they could do to leverage the administrative capabilities of the application.

Under a SaaS model, since there are no tasks to patch, maintain, update, or keep the SaaS system operational, I.T. personnel can allocate time to maximizing their knowledge of the solution. Some of the key areas has been around learning new functions of the product, understand how employees currently utilize the product, and come up with weekly articles or even lunch-and-learn sessions on tips and "did you know" type content. I.T. has become an enabler of getting employees to maximize their use of applications. Employees have typically relegated themselves to just using the features they know of and have used in the past, even though there are better ways of using the tool. With most SaaS applications, new features and functions are added every month or quarter, so even if a knowledge sharing session was done 2 months ago, there may be dozens of new features and functions to share with employees. The best knowledge sharing is done when functionality is not merely shared as features and functions, but how the features and functions can actually be used and leveraged and truly utilized by employees.

And for administrative "backend" improvements, time can be spent by I.T. personnel to intimately understand new security functionality, new monitoring or management features in SaaS-based applications that the organization can leverage to improve the organization's use of an application. Many times there are integrated role-based security features that can be enabled. Or enhancements in an applications monitoring and employee access tracking can help detect unauthorized access, or improve the integrity and data-leakage protection of enterprise content.

So there's more to SaaS-based applications than merely adding users, removing users, modifying content, and doing basic administrative tasks that I.T. dive into and proactively improve user and administrative tasks in the use of SaaS-based applications.

Focusing on Customization of PaaS Model Applications

Another focus for I.T. personnel is shifting IaaS-based applications from running on virtual machines to PaaS or SaaS based applications. As has been described previously, IaaS is not a very efficient model since it requires patching, updating, and traditional I.T. management that organizations really want to eliminate from the I.T. tasks to optimize I.T. operations. Shifting to PaaS or SaaS applications accomplishes this.

I.T. management can allocate time for personnel to assess all running IaaS systems and determine what can be done to shift the applications away from running on virtual machines to running as services. With the identification of systems that could be prioritized for conversion, I.T. can then create a roadmap and spend weeks or months simply stepping through the process of optimizing applications into a more efficient and effective runtime model. This modernization effort could keep I.T. busy for a very long time.

Even after applications have been migrated off IaaS to a PaaS-based model, the continual customization of the application, the optimization of the PaaS-application, and even adding in new features and functions identified during the application suitability step on what will make an application more effective for employees becomes a series of valuable tasks for I.T. to perform.

Enabling More Time to Focus on Monitoring and Security Tasks

With core application optimization, administration optimization, and IaaS to PaaS conversion tasks in progress, I.T. can also focus time on developing and improving best practices for the monitoring and security of the new modernized I.T. environment.

Again, in the past when it took a lot of I.T. time simply to keep servers and systems running, I.T. had little time to proactively improve the operational state of their environment. As mundane tasks have been lifted from I.T. personnel when services are shifted away from internal corporate datacenter applications to hosted SaaS and PaaS based applications, I.T. has been able to focus on monitoring and security tasks to be more proactive in solving potential problems before they occur.

I.T. has shifted from being one of looking behind itself on what has occurred, to being able to look forward on what I.T. can do to facilitate improvements in the organization's use of technology. Monitoring is no longer simply spent looking to identify problems that occurred and reactively respond to the problems, but to monitor current operational states, project out patterns in runtime operations, and script capacity to come online before performance is impacted, and to proactively eliminate capacity (and thus runtime costs) when capacity is not needed.

This powering on and off capacity is something that can be done in cloud-based consumption models that is very different than in the buy / build / run model where capacity is purchased and encumbered whether the capacity is utilized or not. For organizations running systems 60-80 hours a week that can shutdown excess capacity in the other 80-100 hours a week, the organization can save 40-60% of their runtime costs. This is something that could never have been done in the past that, if managed and leveraged by I.T. in this new world of computing, can have significant improvements in lowering costs of I.T. operations on a business.

And with respect to security, for years I.T. has been reactive, addressing security threats when others have been hacked or attacked, following others rather than proactively seeking ways to improve the security stature of the organization. I.T. can maximize integrated tools in SaaS, PaaS, and hosted cloud provider solutions to minimize the impact security threats can have on the organization.

Focusing on End User Productivity

Besides all of the backend enhancements that I.T. can utilize its time doing, there's so much that can be done on the "frontend" in working with employees and their optimization of I.T. that can help to improve business processes. As an organization may have identified and experienced in the strategy planning process interviewing employees and assessing employee usage of applications, there's frequently a disconnect between I.T.'s knowledge of what employees do in a day, and how the tools they use meet (or more likely fail to meet) their needs.

Employees have gotten used to I.T. just telling them to how to "use the applications and tools" rather than really helping to improve their daily tasks and responsibilities through the use of technology. As many organizations have seen and experienced with the adoption of cloud-based file storage and collaboration tools like Box.com, DropBox, or GoogleDocs, employees simply wanted to share and collaborate internally and externally with others. Traditional I.T. fileservers didn't provide this functionality, so employees found a way to do it on their own. The same pent-up demand for other uses of technology exist in employee desire to maximize their use of data, ability to leverage and access information from a mobile device just like Apps allow them to do with other services.

I.T. can shift from a reactive end customer service organization that helps employees fix things when they don't work, to a business entity where I.T. can proactively understand what employees do, and develop systems, tools, and solutions that make I.T. an enabler of technical solutions that help the organization more effectively do their jobs.

Embarking on Data Analysis and Predictive Learning on Opportunities

Lastly, a key area that I.T. has been able to focus its newfound time has been embarking on solutions that maximize data analysis and predictive learning solutions. As social media organizations have leveraged their knowledge of data to understand what consumers have searched for, have bought, and will likely buy into big business, organizations have tools available that enable users to leverage data to the benefit of the organization.

Data analysis tools that can help an organization identify which customers will buy or increase purchases of their goods or services, predictive learning tools that can project inventory demands for better "just in time" production and stocking levels, security analysis proactively learning, predicting, and preventing security threats and data compromise in the environment.

The tools exist, it's just a matter of "someone" in an organization to understand the tools, build models on leveraging the tools, and implement and train frontline employees how to utilize the tools to improve how technology can be a true enabler in the success of the organization.

11 SUMMARY

Cloud scale and Cloud optimization are no longer buzzwords to describe a potential future model for an optimized technology driven model, but years into the introduction of the cloud to the marketplace are now core tenets of technology innovation leveraged by enterprises to their benefit. Technological changes have brought about the vision for change, and application and datacenter modernization is the foundational step that will help organizations maximize their potential for technological optimization.

The goal for application and datacenter modernization isn't to be "all cloud, right now," but to selectively choose what makes most sense for each application and stage the implementation in the enterprise over time in a way that makes the most sense for the organization. Most enterprises will operate in a hybrid model, with some services hosted and running in the cloud, and other services remaining on-premise. The larger the enterprise, the longer the organization will remain in a hybrid state. However, EVERY organization needs to have an Application and Datacenter Modernization roadmap that'll clearly identify how, when, and what applications it will shift to a more optimized model.

For many organizations, simply bundling up virtual machine on-premise and moving them to an IaaS cloud-based virtual machine is the easy first step to dip their toe into the enterprise cloud model. However, running applications on a server, in an operating system is an expensive operational model. The time and effort organizations spend in patching, updating, upgrading, and managing servers is what has driven the movement to SaaS-based applications. Email and Calendaring systems have been broadly adopted and deployed by organizations of all sizes across all industries as email is the same sending and receiving of messages no matter what industry an organization belongs to. A one-to-many model bodes well for email as a service, and organizations have adopted cloud-based email with rapid deployments.

PaaS-based models are the step for applications that require customization unique to an enterprise, but allows for a simplified model that eliminates an organization's need to host servers and manage the core infrastructure of a server environment itself.

This book identified the cost model where transitioning from on-premise applications to a SaaS or PaaS model is not more expensive than the major lift and shift organizations go through every 3-5 years to upgrade and update their applications. Organizations investing in shifting from one major version to another major version of a solution can transition the organization out of an internally hosted model to a shared model that eliminates a huge portion of an organization's cost of I.T. operations.

Early adopters and now mainstream enterprise adopters have enjoyed significant operational benefits in their journey to modernize their applications and datacenters. I.T. personnel no longer spend their time trying to keep systems operational, and instead allocate their time to proactive tasks that enabled I.T. to truly be an enabler for the enterprise.

I.T. can now spend its time helping employees better leverage technology, utilize technology to optimize employee's time in the day, and identify ways to improve security.

It is truly a new world of I.T. with an opportunity for all organizations to modernize their application and datacenter environments, and move the organization into a business model optimize to help the organization meet their business goals and objectives.

ABOUT THE AUTHORS

<u>Rand Morimoto, Ph.D., MBA, CISSP, MCITP:</u> Dr Morimoto is the President of Convergent Computing (CCO), a San Francisco Bay Area based strategy and technology consulting firm. CCO helps organizations development and fine tune their technology strategies, and then provide hands-on assistance planning, preparing, implementing, and supporting the technology infrastructures. CCO works with Microsoft and other industry leading hardware and software vendors in early adopter programs, gaining insight and hands-on expertise to the technologies far before they are released to the general public. This early adopter experience has allowed Rand and CCO's experts develop tips, tricks, and best practices based on lessons learned.

<u>Chris Amaris, MCITP, MCTS, CISSP:</u> Chris is the chief technology officer and cofounder of Convergent Computing. He has more than 30 years' experience consulting for Fortune 500 companies, leading companies in the technology selection, architecture, design, and deployment of complex enterprise cloud integration projects. Chris specializes in leveraging Microsoft Azure and System Center technologies to achieve high degree of on-premise to cloud integration, migration, automation, and self-service, reducing the level of effort and time-to-market for organizations while providing high levels of fault tolerance and availability.

www.ingramcontent.com/pod-product-compliance
Lightning Source LLC
Chambersburg PA
CBHW061032050326
40689CB00012B/2784